THE WOMAN WHO FLUMMOXED THE FAIRIES

An Old Tale from Scotland

Retold by HEATHER FOREST

Illustrated by SUSAN GABER

Harcourt Brace & Company

San Diego   New York   London

Special thanks to Elinor Williams, our editor

Requests for permission to make copies of any part of the work
should be mailed to: Permissions Department,
Harcourt Brace & Company, 6277 Sea Harbor Drive,
Orlando, Florida 32887-6777.
Library of Congress Cataloging-in-Publication Data
Forest, Heather.
The woman who flummoxed the fairies.
Summary: Asked to make a cake for the fairies, a clever bakerwoman
must figure out a way to prevent the fairies from wanting to keep
her with them always to bake delicious cakes.
[1. Cake — Folklore. 2. Folklore — Scotland.]
I. Gaber, Susan, ill. II. Title.
PZ8.1.F76Wo   1990   398.2'1'09411 [E]   88-28448
ISBN 0-15-299150-6
B C D E

The illustrations in this book were done in watercolor, acrylic,
and colored pencil on Coquille board.
The display type was hand lettered by Connie Gustafson Smiley.
The text type was set in Cochin by Thompson Type, San Diego, California.
Color separations were made by Bright Arts, Ltd., Hong Kong.
Printed and bound by Tien Wah Press, Singapore
Production supervision by Warren Wallerstein and Ginger Boyer
Design by Camilla Filancia and Susan Gaber

For Larry, Lucas, and Laurel
— H. F.

For Rich and Elias
— S. G.

Of rainbow wings and baking things, let us tell a tale . . .

Long ago, late at night, when everyone was sleeping, little fairy folk with rainbow wings flew into people's houses. They danced on the dinner tables, perched on the teacups, and feasted on leftover cake crumbs.

Never did they get a taste, however, of the fine cakes made by the bakerwoman who lived at the edge of the forest. *Her* cakes were always eaten down to the last bite.

This made the King of the Fairies furious. "I must have a taste of the bakerwoman's cake!" he raged.

H e sent the fairy folk to hide outside the bakerwoman's window. They hid in the flower petals, they sat on the leaves, they hung from the vines, and they watched and they listened.

One day, they heard her say that she was going to the royal palace to bake a wedding cake for the Princess. She took her finest linen apron from the shelf, bid good-bye to her husband and wee babe, and off she went. "I'll take the short road home through the woods," she said as she left, "and be back this evening as fast as I can!"

The leaves began to rustle, the flower petals opened, and out darted the fairies. They rushed into the deep woods to tell the King of the Fairies that the bakerwoman would pass by the fairy mound on her way home that night.

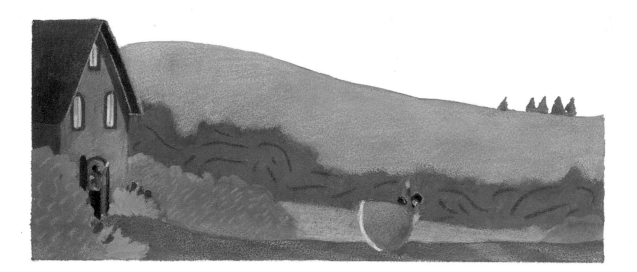

Meanwhile, the bakerwoman arrived at the palace, set to baking, and made a cake that was as tall as she was. When it was done, she took off her apron, folded it carefully, and put it in her pocket. She bid good-bye to the King, the Queen, and the Princess and hurried off to her wee babe at home.

Just as the sun was setting, she entered the deepest, darkest part of the forest. The fairies, like fireflies at twilight, flew around her and blew fern dust in her face. She felt a sleepiness come over her. I cannot take another step, she thought. I must rest. So down she sat on the soft grass of the fairy mound beside the road and closed her eyes.

uddenly, down, down, down she fell and landed flat, splat, on a marble floor. All around her, candles were blazing and fairy folk were flying. The King of the Fairies sat on his tiny golden throne. "I want you to bake us a cake," he said.

Oh, thought the bakerwoman, I cannot do that! If they taste how good my cakes are, they will keep me here in the world of the fairies for all time baking cakes. I'll never see my husband, my wee babe, or my home again!

She quickly gathered her wits about her and thought of a plan. "Very well," she said with a twinkle in her eye. "I'll bake a cake for you."

She took her apron from her pocket and calmly tied it around her waist. She rubbed her hands together and said, "Now, where's the flour and a bowl?"

"We have no flour here," said the King. "But as for a bowl . . ." He reached behind his throne and pulled out a tiny golden bowl the size of a thimble.

"I cannot make a cake in a bowl that won't hold even an egg," she replied. "You must go to my house and get my bowl and the great sack of flour beside the stove."

"Easily said, easily done," said the King. He clapped his hands, he stamped his foot, and the ground split open.

The fairies flew down the dark road through the woods to the bakerwoman's house. They peeked in the window at her husband sitting in the kitchen. So as not to be noticed, they made themselves invisible, and in they went. Just as they were raising the great sack of flour, one fairy said, "Wait, I have seen the bakerwoman put far more than flour into her cakes."

So the fairies scurried off into the pantry, and soon chunks of chocolate, raisins, a pitcher of milk, eggs, butter, cream, sugar, honey, walnuts, and all kinds of fine ingredients floated off the shelves.

Then, just as they reached for the bowl, another fairy asked, "What about something to stir the batter with?" And a spoon and the bowl joined all the fine ingredients as they flew through the kitchen and out the window. The bakerwoman's husband watched in amazement.

Back in the fairy kingdom, all the fairies gathered around as the bakerwoman put the fine ingredients into the bowl. Singing a cheery song, she started to stir the batter. Suddenly she stopped and said, "Wait, I cannot bake a cake without my dog."

"Your dog!" cried the King. "Are you planning to put a dog in the cake?"

"Oh, no," she replied. "My big black dog snores an even snore, and I stir two stirs for every one of his snores. I cannot bake a cake unless my pooch measures the stirring for me. You must go to my house and bring me my dog."

"Easily said, easily done," muttered the King, becoming a bit impatient. He clapped his hands, he stamped his foot, and the ground split open.

The fairies flew back down the dark road through the woods to the bakerwoman's house. They made themselves invisible, and in they went. They found the dog sleeping on the kitchen floor. Just as they were about to lift him up, one fairy said, "Maybe she bakes with a cat as well."

And some of the fairies went for the cat curled peacefully under the table. The cat screeched and the dog snored as they floated into the air and out the window on invisible fairy fingers. The bakerwoman's husband watched in disbelief.

Back in the fairy kingdom, the tiny fairies licked their lips, rubbed their hands, and batted their wings, thinking about the fine cake they would soon taste. The bakerwoman stirred to the dog's even snores, and the cat, wrapped around her leg, purred contentedly. Suddenly the bakerwoman stopped and said, "Wait. I cannot bake a cake when I'm worrying about my child. You must go to my house and bring me my wee babe."

"Easily said, easily done," said the King. "But this is your last request!" He clapped his hands, he stamped his foot, and the ground split open.

The fairies flew back down the dark road through the woods to the bakerwoman's house. They made themselves invisible, and in they went. They found the fat, giggling baby perched on a chair in the corner. Just as they were lifting the child into the air, one fairy said, "What if the child gets hungry?" So out the window floated the fat, giggling baby, a bowl of porridge, and a silver spoon. "Wait! Stop!" cried the baker-woman's husband. He dove out the window and ran into the forest after them.

eep in the woods, the fairy mound opened, and down into the dark hole tumbled the child, the bowl of porridge, and the spoon. The bakerwoman's husband jumped in after them and landed flat, splat, on the marble floor. All around him candles were blazing and fairy folk were flying. His wife was standing in her big white apron. "Thank you, King." She smiled. "I was about to ask for my husband as well!" Then, she whispered to her husband, "Pinch the dog." I wonder, he said to himself, why she wants me to do such a thing? But without a word, he crept over and gave the dog a good, sound pinch, which set the dog howling. The bakerwoman stepped lightly on the cat's tail, which started the cat squalling. All the little fairy folk fell on the floor clutching their ears. For if there's one thing the bakerwoman knew, it's that fairies don't like noise!

In the middle of all the howling, in the middle of all the squalling, she said, "Oh, my poor child must be hungry. Please give the babe that bowl of porridge and the spoon." And the baby began banging the spoon and flinging porridge about.

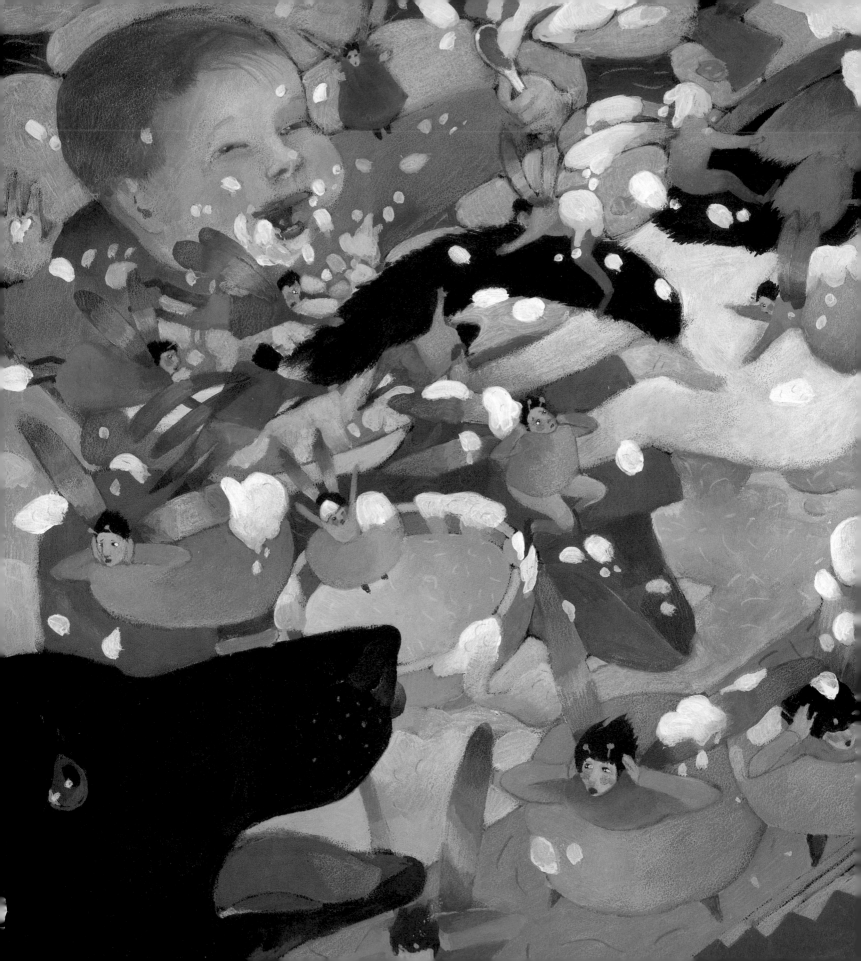

I n the middle of all the howling, in the middle of all the squalling, in the middle of all the banging and flinging, the bakerwoman said, "Where's the oven?"

"Oven?" cried the King, wiping porridge from his rainbow wings. "We have no oven here!" "Well, then," she announced, "you take care of the dog, the cat, and my child, and I'll go home and bake this cake in my own oven."

"No! No!" shouted the King, covering his ears. "Take all of them and their noise home with you!"

"Certainly," she said. "And I'll bring back the cake when it's done. What's more, if you leave me be, I'll bake you a cake whenever you ask for one nicely."

The King clapped his hands, he stamped his foot, and the ground split open.

The bakerwoman grabbed her wee babe and the bowl of batter. Her husband carried the ingredients and the spoon, and with the dog and the cat following, they scurried down the road through the dark woods. And they didn't look back once until they were safe inside their house with the cake baking.

When it was done to a golden brown, the bakerwoman proudly took it out of the oven. Her husband licked his lips at the thought of her good baking, but she took the cake and started toward the door. "Where are you going with that cake?" he asked. "Oh," she replied. "I'm taking it to the fairies as I promised." Bravely she walked down the dark road through the woods to the little green hill and set the cake down. She must have glanced away for a moment, for when she looked back, the cake had vanished. In its place was a chunk of fairies' gold.

The bakerwoman picked up the gold and admired it. She put it in her pocket, but she knew she couldn't keep it just for herself, or it would turn to dust.

For fairies' gold, they say, is like love or knowledge — or a good story. It's most valuable when it's shared.

Author's Note

Centuries ago in Scotland, storytellers who were well known in their communities for the vivid tales they told around the hearth were called seanachies. This retelling of *The Woman Who Flummoxed* the Fairies* is based on a seanachie household tale from Durris near Aberdeen in the Scottish Highlands.

*Flummox is an old word that means to confuse, perplex, surprise, or befuddle.